Poesia

Himangshi Dangle

BookLeaf Publishing

India | USA | UK

Presentation by *BookLeaf Publishing*

Web: www.bookleafpub.com

E-mail: info@bookleafpub.com

ISBN: 9789360947095

First edition 2024

"To the magic that is reading, that takes us to places we've never been."

"To all those who pick up this book, thank you for giving my words a chance."

ACKNOWLEDGEMENT

This journey would not have been possible without the support of my family, professors and mentors, and friends.

To my family, Thank you for encouraging me in all of my pursuits and inspiring me to follow my dreams. I am especially grateful to my parents, who supported me emotionally and financially. I always knew that you believed in me and wanted the best for me. Thank you for teaching me that my job in life was to learn, to be happy, and to know and understand myself; only then could I know and understand others.

I thank my husband for his love, support and guidance. With you, I'm the strongest.

I would like to show my heartfelt gratitude to my teacher Dr. Roopa Shah for encouraging and guiding me in my literary journey in my earlier times.

Finally, thanking BookLeaf Publishing for making this dream come true.

PREFACE

Poetry is like a big ocean and when an individual reads the poetry he or she dives into it extremely deep, so they can understand the reality. After they dive into the poetry, the reader understands the reality and sees the world in a realistic way. As a reader, poetry helps to create an image in their mind and pulls individuals into it which lets them see the world differently and boost their feelings when they are sad or stressed about anything.

This book is a mixture of poetry on varied themes reflecting a different outlook on life. Inspiring avid readers to dream, as dreams do come true only if you work for it anew.

This book is the poet's dream come true!

Life's a Journey

Now, I am boarding a train,
To locate the whereabouts of my brain.

Done to find out my real strength,
What I truly am,
To seek the answers of unspoken,
Unseen mysteries

I am taking this plight,
What I may discover I might,
I am not sure where it ends,
But hoping to learn the new trends.

I am extremely excited and curious!
Although it may be dangerous,
But life's a mystery
And a mystery is always a history!

I am puzzled by the train's route,
From deep dark valleys to distinct
Mountains and high up en route.

I want this journey to be an adventure,
Although it's a venture!
I have boarded this train alone,
So I don't want to be forlorn.

Now, I have completed half of my journey,
So much I have learnt and seen,
It is difficult to say it clean,
All the unimaginable dreams coming true,
Just like it was then with the Bru

My cup's half empty,
Want to fill it with plenty,
Discover the life till the end,
So that we can have a blend.

I still have to complete this trail,
It's not easy as a mail!
Just want to say it friends,
This is not where the imagination ends!
This is not where the imagination ends!!

The infallible

The one who fell every time
Knew how to get back up
No matter how many times
Just grew up

All that falling
Was me growing
No more ashamed of the falling
My wings are just spreading

Stood like a mountain
The infallible
That's all
Even if I have to crawl
I will not brawl

No matter how many times I fall
I will always stand tall

Broken wings

I still remember where I was born,
I still regret that day for long.

So happily I had come out of my shell,
Hoping to see the world with my own eyes and
yell!
Aiming to fly high up in the sky,
So high that I would touch the moon's eye.

Fly to the farthest land and distant seas,
That no one could ever see.

I was just waiting for my wings,
To try out different things,
Once I had those wings,
I was a free bird in new innings.

And all those thoughts went wrong,
All the little dreams were crushed,
Which hoped to fly along,
May be I had rushed?

But was that wrong?
To experience the world with my own eyes,
Because yours was full of sighs.

A thought struck her so hard,
Had I grown up to be a retard?
To believe in others' experiences and trust their
opinions.

Don't I have opinions of my own?
Oh god! I should have known.

The wings were broken before the first flight,
But was that the end of the road?
The broken wings still hope to fly one day,
Because you don't need wings to fly,
Until your faith is high.

Demons

My demons never hide
They lay out in plain sight
Don't be scared of them
Face them upright
Don't worry they don't bite

They will play
When they feel being played
They will stay
If you let them stay
They will leave
As soon as you don't feed
They don't have any greed

They attack
Only when they are attacked
They love
If felt loved
They care as they sense care
They hide in their lair

They will stay there
Unless awakened by your flair
My demons are rare
Only because they care
And they are fair
Though they will stare
They will always share

Plans

Plan A plan B plan C
I don't know what the future holds for me
But I'm gonna be me
Upcoming events can't see
Let loose your worries free
This is the moment to be
A treasure to hold
Make it gold
Take this road
You are not that old
Life's not a shape to mould
Nor take any as told
Even if they scold
Come on be bold
It's your decision to hold
The power is untold
See the paths that unfold
That's how you roll
To reach your goal
And once you are done
This is not the end
There is a lot to comprehend
Break yourself again to mend
Somethings never end
But don't bend
Don't pretend

Just understand
Plans don't work out till the end
But you will still make it my friend

Partner

I need you in my team
Correct me when I'm wrong
Support me in the storm
With you I'll be strong

Be with me for long
Just like a song
Be my words
To sing along
With you I want to belong
Tell me if I'm wrong
I feel this all along

I was so scared to love
With you I'm no more
Be my sea I'll be your shore
I don't want anything else anymore
Be my peace I'll be your home

I don't want to be alone
My little gnome
With you I'll roam
From Spain to Rome

I just need you to be close
You are the one I chose
I don't want to overdose
You're my rose
I'm high on oxytocin, dopamine and serotonin
It's just I'm feelin'

Be with me in this game
I'll take your name
Be my knight I'll be your dame
This train has got no chain
I'll be with you in the rain
Be my heart I'll be your brain
Life will play its game
We just have to aim
I'll be your partner just the same

Traitor

I have been thinking
With this feeling sinking

If you ever take me for granted
That's the last thing I wanted
So many times I have been taunted
Now I am just astounded
Always I have been grounded

Shouldn't have stayed this way,
Shouldn't have loved you anyway
Shouldn't have trusted your say
Now I'm in dismay.

I wanted you to stay
Now that you are away
Took me for granted anyway
It's not a game to play
You have lost me anyway

You lost a diamond for a dime
Yes it is a crime
I hate to share what's mine
I promised you a lifetime
And you couldn't stay mine

Not ashamed of your sin
Since when did you begin
Says your grin
There is a traitor within...

Not your valentine

Don't love me for a single day
Instead love me everyday

I won't be your Valentine
Don't need your gifts
Just your time
All I know is that you are mine
So don't behave like a swine

Don't take me for granted
Was all I wanted
Nothing I have ever demanded

Unless you learn to address
It will be a mess
Say and act like you are mine

Till then I won't be your Valentine.....

Thank you

I would like to thank you
To show me the way
And that's all I can say
It's up to you to stay
Life's a dismay
It's your array
You got away
To find the way
I hope you find what you may
Even if you have to fray
Just remember you're a ray
Just shine along the way
Because they need to know
You are the one to glow
Just learn and grow
This boat has to row
Into the unknown

Masterpiece

Turning my pain into art
I'm about to start
Rather than falling apart
With all my heart
I'm gonna turn into an art

Need to keep things in check
Even if I'm a wreck
What the heck
There's a pain in my neck

So let's just start
and create art
You are a masterpiece
With all the crease
With so much ease

Don't be worried oh please
You are imperfectly perfect
Let them introspect

Zindagi

Zindagi ki bhaag daud me
Agar thak jao toh rukna sahi hai
Ruk kar sochna ki harna nahi hai
Kyunki manzil ab door nahi hai
Agar maan lo haar
Laut kar yahin ana hai mere yaar
Tumhari takat vishwas aur himmat me hi hai
Girna uthna parna chalna
Yahi to zindagi hai
Agar muskuraye hue zamana ho gaya
Toh ab bahana mil gaya
Jashn manao iss zindagi ka
Rone ke mauke kai hain
Zindagi ek rasta hai
Bas chalte jana hai
Aur safar ka lutf uthate jana hai

Diwali

Diwali is the festival of lights
It's celebrated because Lord Rama conquered his
right
Also, the wrong lost from the right.

We lit the diyas to elevate the darkness and not
to make a mess!
We burst crackers of fire
In India, every year the pollution gets higher!

Will it continue till ages & ages?
Because that's not what was taught by the sages!

Endangering your own life and of others,
Does that really bothers?
Yes it does,
Life's more precious.

Don't waste money on crackers,
Instead help the poor man
Who is struggling for his basic needs,
Follow this trend,
Oh my dear friend!!!

Koshish

Hum apna haal-e-dil kavitaon se bayan karte
hain
Aur wo humse keh gaye ki aap likhti bahut
achha hain

Wo kehte hain ki hamari baatein sachhi lagti
hain
Kyunki likhte waqt hum sochte nahi
Jo mehsoos karte hain wahin bayaan karte hain
Sach hi toh kagaz pe bayaan karte hain

Iss nasamjhi ke daur mein
samajhdaari hamari aisi hai
Jante hain ki hum tumhare ho nahi sakte
Isiliye koshish bhi nahi karni hai
Kyunki ladai apno se hogi
Jin pe humne apni jaan waari hai

Ek din jagmaga uthenge jugnu ki tarah
Qki mehnat ki raatein kai hain
Baatein banane wale bhi bahut honge
Magar saath dene wale kaafi hain
Kardenge dariyaan paar
Koshish zaari hai
Mehnat karne ki poori taiyari hai

Aap saath de ya na de
Aap jaan hamari hain
Apne sapne sach karne ki ab hamari baari hai
Ab hamari baari hai

Aatmavishwas

Inn aansuon ko bahne mat dena
Inhe apni takat banao
Shabdo ke yudhh mein
Inhe apni dhaal banao
Kyunki waqt aagaya hai ladai ka
Hum aurantein hain! Kamzor hain!
Inn vicharo ko nasht karne ka yahi samay hai!

Chhod do iss sansar ka vichar
Jisme tumhare vicharo ka koi mol nahi
Jo hume dharma ki baatein sikhaye
Wohi khud kyun bhool jaaye?

Bahut ho gayi ab chuppi
Ab bolne ka samay aaya hai
Apne shastron ko uthao behno
Kyunki sawal ab apne atmasaman ka hai

Tum apni madhur boli se chedo ye saaz
Uthake apni awaz
Kehdo ye raaz
'Humse hai zamana
Zamane se hum nahi'

Jo insaan apni Dharti Ma ki raksha na kar paya
Wo hamari kya karega?

Aatmanirbhar hona seekho sakhiyon!

Tum akeli hi ladd sakti ho
Iss duniya se
Zara atmavishwas toh badhao
In aansuon ko bahne mat dena
Inhe apni takat banao

Broken heart

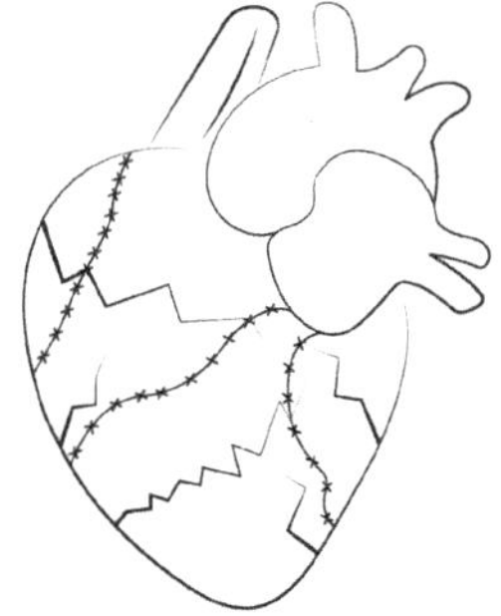

I see the essence of me in you
And yes that's true

You're the rain, I'm the dew
You're the broken part, I am the glue
Our relationship is out of the blue

Because no one knew
But it still exists in my view
I know people like us are very few
You're the dream that I want to pursue
Your face is what I drew
My feelings for you grew
But I couldn't find you

I am waiting so long in the queue
Our bond needs a sew
Let the colour flourish in hue

It's definitely not a jew
So let's just renew

Our story will have a review
I just wish you knew
You left me in a stew
I shouldn't or should I continue?
I wish you knew
My broken heart will always wait for you

Time

Time is now or never,
And once it is gone, gone forever,
Once you missed it, the chance is never.

Time! Time! Time!
Once the clock stricks nine,
Have your dinner and go to bed,
Rather watching your idiot box instead.

I am still missing my childhood days,
It has gone as it has been ages,
Where is that time now?
Is it really we have changed or the time?
We have to adapt to the changes to be fine.

Only the fittest survives,
Don't know what next arrives!
Still time runs ahead of our lives,
It's time to win against time.

Because life will not stop,
It goes on and on,
The lesson that always learnt by time,
'A stitch in time saves nine!'

It is always said that,
'Prevention is better than cure'.
But time has still not found out any medicine for
that cure!
It is we have to stand up straight,
And face the challenges upright.

In some states, there are still no slates,
Oh god! Why are we so late?
It is time to wake up
To create a democracy for all.

Wafa

Janab
Wafa ka wafa se saath do
Bewafa toh har koi hai yahan
Tum buss mujhe apna haath do
Agar bigad jaaye kabhi waqt mera
Tum buss mere saath raho
Halat ache ho ya bure
Tum yoonhi paas raho

Dekho kabhi humse na naraz raho
gussa hi sahi
Baat kar liya karo
Agar ruth jau toh mana liya karo
Tumhari hi hoon
Zara samajh liya karo

Hai pyaar tumse, saath yunhi diya karo
Meri wafa ko wafa se kiya karo

The pain

The sight of people begging on the street
Gives me immense pain,
Who is to blame?
Poverty is such a disease,
It doesn't let you live with ease.

It leaves people half alive half dead,
They can't even afford a bed!
Malnutrition is on the rise,
The prices of goods touching up the skies.

How will the poor survive?
They are not bees to live in hives!
They are humans after all,
Needing food, shelter, water and some pride.

Why differentiate them into classes?
World is full of masses,
World has enough place to accommodate all,
That's why it's round like a ball!!

Help the poor as much as you can,
Deeds won't go waste Oh Man!
Understand the life of the Poor,
Just be the doer!!

Believe in 'I can change'
If I can change then you can change
If you can change we will surely change!!

Water

Water is a fact of matter,
Which cannot be in the latter,
If not used properly,
It will be left barely.

Crisis of water is scarcity,
Which is found almost in all city,
Water is the basis for life.
A day will come when you'll have to strife.

To stop this we have to strive,
We have to stay alive,
Conservation of water is our prime,
Wasting it would be a crime!

Forgiveness

I know you are mad at me
And you have all the reasons to be
Mad at me
You are free
And I agree

But I want you to see
Amidst all the anger
It's just dumb me
In love with you completely
Asking for forgiveness
To be
I know I'm a mess
Yes I do stress

All I seek is forgiveness
With you I'm blessed
Honey please don't stress
Give me a chance to progress
I'll make it right
With all my might
Keep it in sight
To avoid such fights
Baby you are right

Just bless me with forgiveness

I did it

I did it
With my pace
And no race
I did it
Like an ace
With all the craze
I did it
Look on my face
Is all it says
I did it
With all the grace
All of my days
I'm in my own space
Just with my grace
I did it
I'm so amazed

To the Finishing line

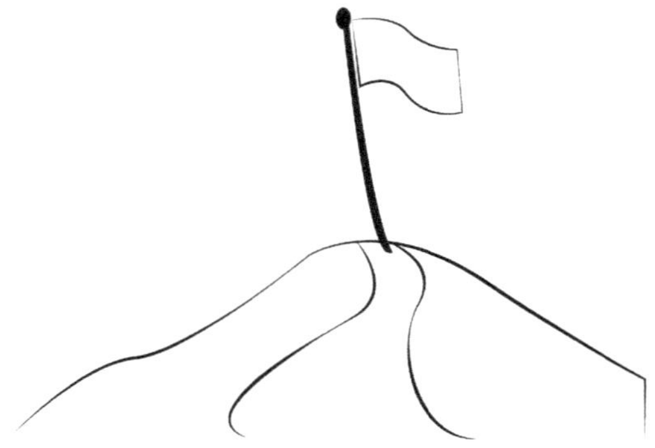

Get up it's a race!
It was in my good old days
Run in this race
Was the craze
And I was amazed
We got up and ran in a haze

But all this running made me think
All the years passed by in a blink
All gone in a wink
Study for the test
Work like pest
Forget the rest
To be the best
Put the strain on the brain
Everything is going down the drain

Missed all the rain
Now it's just the pain
Running and hoping to win
It's a race to begin
Racing just for acing
What about the stress we are facing?
Was it worth chasing?
Though dreams are worth the chase
Not at the cost of your grace
Just do it at your own pace
To the finishing line, it's a race!

Heart of stone

My heart has become a stone
It is all gone
I looked for it everywhere
Now it's in a despair

It was bold
But all the hurt made it cold
It has been broken, lied and played
But still it stayed
It only prayed
Alas it strayed

Tried to heal it every day
Cared too much anyway
Slowly slowly turned into a rock
All the pathways were blocked
Don't be so shocked

Now, no hurt can mock
It's all locked

A little less hate
Could have turned its fate
It's my heart at stake
Not my mistake
Leave it alone for my sake
I'm on a break!
Give love and love you take
Heart of stone is hard to break!

Pyaar nahi

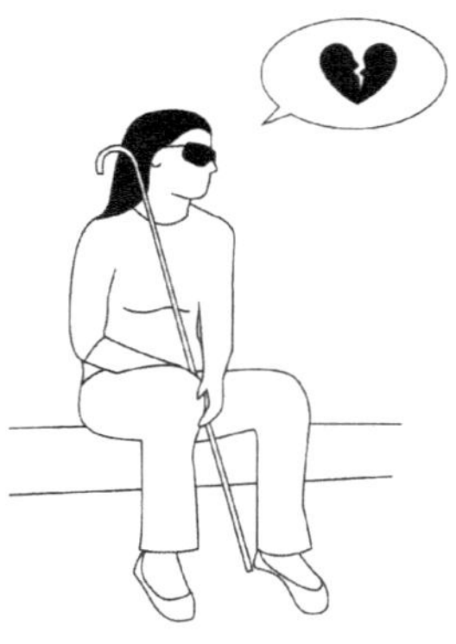

Pahle to tumhare jhooth par bhi bharosa tha
Ab tumhare sach par bhi yakeen nahi
Aankhon par mandra raha dhuaan
Ab gayab saa ho raha ho gaya hai
Fareb ab dikhai dene laga hai

Tumhari baaton par aitbaar nahin
Yoonnhi karte raho nazar andaz humein
Jaa ab tujhe pyaar nahi
Wo mera yaar nahi
Kehti rahi baar baar wahi
Tumne sunna hi nahi
Jaa ab tujhse pyaar nahi…………..

Strong

They said you are too strong
You don't belong
I know, that's when I'm not wrong

My firewall is too strong
No place for your fire
Won't act as per your desire
I'm not a crier
I'm strong with my fire

Been like this since ages
Fill up all the pages
Been through every stages
Broken all the cages
Handled all the rages

Don't be mistaken by my kindness
I don't guess
I know my value
I know my worth
You can't buy me with dearth

I don't bend
Nor pretend
I just mend
Don't follow the trend
I always comprehend

So sorry I'm not a follower
Only a believer
There is nothing wrong with being strong
I don't right all the wrongs
So let them say what they want
Let them taunt
You just let your talent flaunt
You just let your talent flaunt